ADVENTURES OF GREENLAND

NEHA KEDIA

ISBN 979-888530660-7

Greenland was a beautiful kingdom hidden deep amidst the forest and mountains. The land was home to Ogres, Giants, and human fairies. Human fairies are people born out of human and fairy parents, so they also had a few magical powers but not as great as the fairies.

This kingdom was ruled by a human fairy king with his queen and all the ogres, giants, and human fairies abided by their rules.

Since these special people were related to fairies whenever a child is born, they were assigned to a fairy godmother, and it was the duty of the fairy God Mother to protect the child and bless them.

Eva was a cute little girl born into the family and she was assigned with a fairy God Mother called Irish. The God Mother Irish saw Eva and the moment she picked Eva up, Eva started to cry.

Irish felt that such a beautiful child should never cry and gifted her with the feeling of no sorrow which meant Eva would never feel sad. Eva's mother felt it was a great gift and started to dance with joy.

Years passed and Eva turned 6 years old. Due to the blessing, she felt no sorrow even when she fell, got hurt, or even when someone was suffering in front of her.

Eva's father fell sick and died which broke Eva's and her mother's heart, but in spite of all this Eva felt no sorrow.

Now the blessing which made her mother dance started to seem like a curse. And Eva too hated it as she began to grow up.

Once Eva turned 18 years old, she asked her mother how she could get rid of this blessing since she did not want to be someone who felt no sorrow with things even when they broke her heart.

Her mother replied, only the Fairy God Mother Irish could take away the gift, but she lives on top of the mountain which is also home to Ogres and Giants who are forbidden from stepping into Greenland by the ruling king.

Eva was determined to get rid of this gift, so she decided to climb the mountain to meet her fairy Godmother. Eva's mother was too weak to accompany Eva, so Eva set out on the journey all alone.

Once she reached the foot of the mountain, Eva was very scared since it seemed to be very dense, deep, and dark.

But she had to keep herself strong, so she started to climb up. After climbing for a few days, Eva reached the mountain area which was occupied by the Ogres. She started to keep an eye and climb carefully up. Suddenly her leg slipped, and she fell rattling a lot of stones and making a huge noise.

The moment she opened her eyes she found herself surrounded by Ogres, and Eva got scared and screamed.

The ogres then asked her what was she doing there, did not she know that Ogres are banished from Greenland and so are human fairies from the mountains?

Eva insisted on meeting her fairy godmother who lived on the top of these mountains. Ogres laughed and told her they will not allow her to pass from there.

Eva explained that she is blessed with the feeling of no sorrow and had to get it changed. The Ogres laughed and told her that is the best gift she had, and she will not suffer ever. Suddenly they noticed that due to the fall Eva had hurt herself badly and was bleeding still she was standing normal.

It surprised the Ogres and asked her to sit down so that they could help her with the wound. It was a large wound for a human fairy. So, ogres allowed her to stay with them till her wounds healed.

While Eva was staying with Ogres, she would try to help them in all possible ways, play with their kids. Due to her cheerful nature, she started to spread happiness all around them.

Finally, the Ogres' hearts melted with Eva's gestures, and they accepted her as a friend. That night Ogres told the story of how the current king and queen have thrown the Ogres and Giants out of Greenland and mistreated them. Also, they were forced to do free labor.

Eva due to her gift could not feel the sorrow of the Ogres but she knew it was wrong and must be changed. She promised she will try to help them and make Human fairies, Ogres, and Giants live together.

The next day Eva was ready to climb the mountain further. The Ogres gave her a big metal vessel made by them and the Giants really liked them. They asked Eva to give them to the giants which would make them happy and that they would also be assured that we trust you.

Eva was excited and at the same time nervous too for the next part of her journey. She started to climb ahead. After a few days of climbing, she reached a part of the mountain where the trees were taller and denser.

Giants could smell her in the air and came searching for her, they looked terribly angry and asked what she was doing there. Eva quickly took out the vessel which the Ogres has gifted to her, the giants were surprised to see the vessel made by Ogres with a human fairy.

They asked Eva if she had stolen them from the Ogres to which Eva replied no and told them why she was there and how Ogres had gifted Eva the vessel so that giants could allow Eva to pass and meet her fairy God Mother.

Giants knew stealing vessels from Ogres was impossible, but they were surprised that despite ill-treatment by Human Fairies how could the Ogres trust Eva.

But the giants had to obey the rules made between them which allowed anyone carrying an Ogre vessel to pass through the Giant's land. The giants took the vessel from Eva and allowed her to pass on.

Eva was overly excited as she was about to complete the last part of her journey and could finally meet her fairy Godmother.

She began to climb the mountain and after a few days of hard struggle, she reached the house of the fairy God Mother which was on the top of the mountains.

Eva knocked on the door, but no one opened it so she asked if anyone was inside but there was no response.

Eva tried to look inside but could not see anything, so she waited the entire day, ate fruits from the trees, and slept on the veranda.

The next day she again knocked and waited for someone to come back or open the door.

This went on for a week and after a week of waiting, Eva again went to knock on the door. This time the moment she touched the door, the door opened, and Eva was shocked.

She was scared but still mustered the courage and stepped inside and bang! The door closed behind her.

Gathering courage Eva stepped inside the house, and the moment she stepped inside the entire house Enlighted with lights and in front, she was smiling-her fairy God Mother Irish.

Eva asked Irish why she did not open the door when she was inside, she had been knocking on the door and staying outside the door for the last few days.

Fairy God Mother smiled and answered that it was a test for those who came to visit her. If they needed her, they would wait and stay here for days until the door was open or she was turned back. Eva has passed the test, so the door has opened now.

Fairy God Mother served Eva hot food and warm clothes. After Eva changed and had a hearty meal, Fairy God Mother asked her to rest and said that they would speak tomorrow about the reason behind her visit.

Eva was very tired she laid down on the cozy bed and fell asleep immediately. In the morning Eva was fresh and happy.

After breakfast, Fairy God Mother asked her the reason for her surprise visit. Eva requested fairy God Mother to take back the gift of no sorrow. Irish was surprised that someone can ask her to take away the gift, for her not feeling sorrow the best gift a human fairy could ask for.

But Eva told she wanted to feel sadness when something went wrong with her near and dear ones and for others so that she can reach out and help more people. Irish was happy to hear that, she agreed to take away the gift of no sorrow from Eva and assured Eva that she would always be there to help her whenever Eva needed her fairy God Mother.

Eva thanked Irish and she started to walk back home. On her way back home, she again met the Giants, and they offered her refreshments and also a place to rest.

Eva was thankful to them and sat down with them and they started to talk about the past how they used to live in Greenland and enjoyed their life there. But the current king and queen banished them from Greenland and made them slaves to work on their *farms. The giants who worked were chained and often beaten even for small mistakes. Since the giants were very less in number and the army was too huge with arms and ammunition, they were not able to protect them.*

Eva said that human fairies were made to believe that giants had been killing and eating them if they found them alone and harmed them in ways, which had made them scared of the giants.

The giants said that they were false stories spread by the Queen and King to banish the Giants and snatch their land which was the most fertile land in the kingdom.

This saddened Eva very deeply and she assured the Giants that she would do her best to help them.

Later Eva said Goodbye to the Giants and move down. On the way she stopped to meet Ogres. The Ogres also welcomed Eva like a friend and Eva was also happy to see them. The swamps did not bother Eva and she enjoyed playing with the kids.

Later she sat down with the Ogres and they also told they used to live in other parts of Greenland with their families which was a large Swamp part of Greenland, they were very happy and enjoyed staying there, at times some human fairies used to pass by and they loved to check and buy vessels made by the Ogres since near the swamps was a large mine from which Ogres used to collect metal and used to make vessels from them.

But the King and Queen banished them from Greenland and passed the order to shoot the Ogres at the site.

After the Ogres left, the King captured the place along with the mines.

Eva said human fairies were made to believe that Ogres had started to expand and capture the land forcefully from the human fairies, so it had become necessary to throw them out of Greenland.

The Ogres disagreed and told that this was again a false story to justify the wrongdoings by King and Queen.

Eva understood and saw how difficult it was for Ogres to live on mountains with so few swamps and very tiny houses. The plantation and trees were a little scare on the mountain where they dwelled.

Eva did know how but she was determined to help both the Ogres and the Giants.

Eva started to climb down and reached home. Her mother was happy to see Eva back safe. She told her mother all about her adventure and how the Ogres and Giants were kind to her.

After that, she kept visiting Ogres and Giants often, sometimes alone and sometimes with her mother. The people in Greenland started to know about Eva meeting Giants and Ogres. They started to come to meet her and ask questions about it and she would explain to them how she found them friendly and harmless. Now, human fairies who were curious and excited to know about them asked Eva if they too could visit them.

Eva asked the Ogres and Giants for permission, and they agreed with the only condition that Eva should always accompany them. Slowly 1 or 2 human fairies started to visit the Ogres and Giants and confirmed what Eva used to say about them and later more joined in.

People started to become friends with Ogres and Giants and the news of this friendship started to spread. It reached the palace of King and Queen. They were not at all pleased to hear the news since they had spread the fear only to keep human fairies away from Giants and Ogres. It helped them to torture them and capture their share of land in Greenland.

The Queen summoned her faithful servant Candy and asked her to arrange to take Eva to the mountains where she would make sure Eva is killed.

Candy went to meet Eva. He told her that he had heard about her friendship with Ogres and Giants which had made him curious, so he also wanted to see them himself.

Eva was happy that another human fairy wanted to be friends with the Ogres and Giants, so she started preparing for the journey. It surprised candy that how can she be so foolish not to ask any questions and trust someone unknown.

Candy and Eva both left for the mountains and as they were climbing up, on the way, there was waiting for Simba the Ogre who did not like the new friendship between Ogres and humans.

Simba has come to kill Eva so that the friendship between her and Ogres could end.

So, he brought a poisonous snake with him to kill Eva. Candy knew about the plan, so he asked Eva to stop and rest there, as he wanted to freshen up and needed a few minutes.

Eva sat down on a nearby stone and once Candy was

out of the side, Simba left the angry hungry snake and the snake rushed towards Eva to bite her.

The moment Eva saw the snake coming towards her, she did not panic she took out a small bowl and milk which she was carrying for the journey and kept it in front of the snake.

The snake had been starving for a few days seeing the milk her quickly started to drink the milk and finished it.

When Simba saw this, he was furious, so he took a huge stone to throw at Eva. But the snake saw Simba throwing a stone at Eva and bit Simba instead of Eva.

The snake bit Simba and disappeared. Simba fell with a huge cry and thrash fell down the stone. Quickly Eva rushed to see what had happened and she saw that Simba is bitten by the snake. She tied a cloth near the bite and told Simba she will come back with help soon. She ran towards the swamps and quickly got all Ogres for help. They quickly took Simba back in swamps and rescued him.

No one knew that Simba was trying to kill Eva except Candy. Candy was back and he was disappointed to see Eva alive. He sent a message to the queen about the escape. but Simba told he will never try to kill her again and all human fairies are not bad. He will welcome them with an open heart.

After that Eva introduced Candy to all Ogres who were very friendly and kind to him. It surprised even Candy because he thought all Ogres were dirty and mean.

The next day Eva said Goodbye to the Ogres and moved ahead to meet the Giants along with Candy.

The queen received the message and immediately summoned Rava the Giant, he was one of the Giants who was caught by the Queen's man and made to work on their fields chained.

The queen told her about Eva and asked him to kill her. She told Rava that if he killed Eva, the queen would free Rava and if he failed, she would punish him with death.

So Rava went on the mountain to search for Eva. Rava stopped Eva and Candy by then he was very hungry and angry. The moment he saw them, Rava shouted today I will have a feast I will eat both of you. He captured both Rava and Candy. Then he told I am very hungry so first I will eat the fatter one of you. Candy got scared and Eva told him please do not eat him, he had come to the mountains because of her words. I told him Giants can be trusted so he came *along with me. If you are hungry, you can eat me.*

Hearing this both Rava and Candy were surprised, they both had been trying to kill Eva, and here Eva was ready to die to save another human's life.

Rava realized Eva was not like the King and Queen or their men. she was a kind-hearted good human fairy. So, he decided to let her go.

After that Rava, Candy, and Eva all three walked together and reached the Giants. The Giants were happy to see Rava back. Also, they welcomed Candy and they all had a pleasant evening. But Candy kept on feeling guilty for his deeds.

He knew has not been honest with Eva. Her kindness had changed his heart. After all the giants had gone to sleep, Candy asked Eva to accompany her a little far since he wanted to talk to her.

Eva was surprised but she could see that Candy looked worried. So, she agreed.

Once they had reached a safe distance from the ears of the Giants, Candy confessed to Rava about him being a soldier and how the Queen had been trying to get her killed.

Eva asked why the Queen wanted her dead. Candy told all about the way the King and Queen captured the lands and mines of Giants and Ogres. They feared that if their secret will be out people will stop following them and they will make Eva their Queen.'

Eva laughed and told she had no intention of becoming a queen and that she just wanted all creatures in Greenland to live together in peace and harmony. She forgave Candy for his mistakes, and they became friends forever.

Rava went to the King and the queen and informed them that he will not kill Eva as she was a kind-hearted human fairy.

This made the queen terribly angry; she commanded her soldiers to capture Rava. She said that Rava would be put to death punishment tomorrow morning for disobeying.

So Rava was caught and put behind bars. He knew his fate but was happy that he did not kill Eva and she would Definity try the giants to get what was rightfully there.

Meanwhile, the news of Rava's death punishment reached the mountains and Eva knew it was because he had failed to kill her.

Eva decided to go to the kingdom and save Rava. She started to get ready for the journey. The giants wanted to accompany her, but they were too huge and would be easily visible before they could even reach the kingdom or make plans to free Rava.

Candy asked Rava if she have any plans for rescuing Rava. Eva refused but she told she did not have any idea as of now but was going to meet Fairy God Mother for her advice. Quickly Eva and Candy started their journey to meet the fairy godmother but before they could go, the Giants asked them the time was very less, let them pick them up and drop them outside the cottage of the Fairy Godmother.

Then they climbed on the Giant and with quick steps, she took them to the cottage of fairy godmother and stood outside along with candy.

Eva knocked and the door opened immediately. Eva stepped inside and hugged Irish. Irish was happy to see Eva there. Then asked her the reason for her visit. Eva told her about what has happened till now and how Rava was caught and killed for not following the order of the Queen.

*Eva asked Fairy God Mother to suggest to her the way
she could rescue Rava without putting anyone's life
in danger.*

*Fairy God Mother thought about it and told me I
have sleeping smoke which can spread everywhere
and make any human fairy smell it fall asleep. Eva
was excited and sad at the same time. She said if it
makes all human fairies sleep how can she carry and
spread it.*

*It was impossible for giants and Ogres to enter the
kingdom unnoticed, Fairy Godmother told Eva she
has a special scarf which if Eva tied around her nose
would not allow the smoke to enter.*

*Eva took the scarf and the bottle of smoke from the
fairy godmother and left, thanking her for helping
her.*

*Irish told she was happy to help Eva and was proud
of her for being so kind-hearted.*

*Eva came out and told the plan to Candy and Giant.
Candy told him he will accompany her since he knew
the path of the kingdom and the prison where the
giants are locked-up with the scarf and different
clothes no one would recognize him.*

It was agreed that the giant will drop them to the outskirts of Greenland so that they can easily walk inside and reach the kingdom from the secret path suggested by Candy.

Once Eva and Candy reached the middle of the kingdom, they opened the bottle given by the fairy God Mother and within minutes it spread all over the kingdom. All the human fairies fell asleep.

Quickly they both went to the prison where the giants were locked. Candy took the keys and opened the cage where Rava and other Giants were locked.

Rava was surprised to see Eva take the risk to save him. Quickly they all left the kingdom and went back to the mountains. Rava and all the giants were thankful to Eva.

The next day in the kingdom when the King, Queen, and soldiers woke up, they found the giants have been liberated from the prison, the queen got furious. Immediately she knew this was the Eva who had dared to free the captives.

The Queen decided it was high time to teach Eva a lesson before she became too famous and come to claim the throne.

King and Queen had their wedding anniversary next month for which they had been planning a party. The queen suggested that she would also call Eva for the party and find a way to kill her.

The next day an invite was sent to Eva. When she read the invite Eva got excited, she thought the queen had realized her mistake and wanted to be friends with her.

Candy tried to warm her, but Eva told her she had to talk to the Queen. So, Candy decided to help Eva, he asked the giants to tie him tight with ropes for the night so that he got marks on his body by morning.

In the morning candy got himself released and went back to Kingdom. The king and queen asked candy where he had been for the last few days. Candy showed his marks and told him the giants had captured him. Somehow, he was realized last night.

The Queen believed him and asked him to rest. Meanwhile, the Queen called her sorcerer and ask him to prepare a poison which she could use on Eva.

The sorcerer prepared a magic portion to be poured on Eva's bed before she arrived, and she would slowly start falling sick with it and die in one month.

The next day Candy came to visit king and queen, and asked he was feeling better is there was any work in which he could help.

The King asked him to prepare for the party planned for the next day and guests would start arriving soon. Soon the guest started to arrive, and he got busy welcoming them. He saw Eva also arrive and pretended not to notice her much.

The guests changed and all arrived in the ballroom for a magnificent party. The palace, the King, and queen guests all dazzled. The party was filled with music, food, drinks, laughs. Eva met the King and Queen, but she did not get a chance to speak to them about the Ogres and Giants. Later she too got carried away and enjoyed the party a lot. Exhausted she went to sleep.

The next day there was the departure of all the guests, along with them Eva also went back home. Candy was surprised that no attempt was made to harm her. Later Candy went to meet the king and queen, they both complimented him for managing the party well. After that Candy asked the queen about not attempting to get rid of Eva.

The queen laughed and told Eva would die soon; he should stop worrying about her. Then she talked about the magic potion that was used to make the bed for Eva. Candy was shocked to hear about it. Then he told the king that he was feeling exhausted due to his injury and needed to rest for a few days.

They allowed Candy to take leave and relax for a few days and asked him to go home. Candy pretended to go home and once he reached home, he disguised himself and come out from a secret passage of his house. He climbed on his horse to rush and meet Eva.

Candy reached Eva's home, where he found only Eva's mother since Eva had gone to meet the Ogres and Giant. He rushed to climb the mountains and reached Ogres as fast he could. But by the time he reached them, Eva had moved on to meet Giants. Ogres informed Candy that Eva looked weak, when asked she told it must be because she was tired.

Ogres offered to carry up to meet the Giants, Candy climbed on one of the Ogres and he climbed as fast he could.

By the time they reached Giants, Eva had become weak and unable to get up from bed. She and giants thought she has fallen sick. They tried to treat her with medicines that they had but Eva's health kept on deteriorating. Candy and Ogre reached Giants and informed them about the poison. The Giants suggested getting Godmother Irish to help.

Candy climbed up with the Giant to bring Irish. The

moment Irish heard about Eva's health, she quickly packed some medicines, and poof they all reached the Giant's place to Eva.

Quickly Irish gave medicines to Eva. Immediately Eva felt relaxed and slept off.

After one full day, Eva got up fresh and fully cured.

Irish said that the King and Queen should be taught a lesson. The news spread that Eva has passed away due to illness. Hearing the news, the King and Queen were happy and celebrated their victory.

Candy and Eva traveled in the night in disguise and reached the kingdom. Irish gave some magical powers to Eva and Candy knew all the secret doors of the palace.

Later when the queen was getting ready to go to sleep near her mirror suddenly, she saw Eva staring at her, she got scared and the moment she turned around no one was there. The queen got scared.

After that, she kept seeing Eva here and there. The moment she would turn to see or call for others she would vanish. The queen started to fall sick and talked about this to the king. The king asked his men to look around, but no one found anyone. Candy told *he knew fairy God Mother of mountains she could help us cure the Queen.*

The King summoned Irish to come immediately. The fairy Godmother came and told the king it is the spirit of Eva that was troubling Queen because she has died too early before her time.

The king asked Irish to help them. Irish explained that the spirit can only go away if the wrongdoing can be corrected, and the last wish of the dead person fulfilled.

So Irish said if the King and queen will accept Eva's last wish and accept Ogres and Giants in Greenland back and if the Queen asks for forgiveness at Eva's grave with a magical flower which Irish had, Eva will be alive again.

The King and Queen immediately agreed. The Ogres and Giants were released from the prison and their lands were returned to them.

Meanwhile, Eva traveled back home and laid down on a special glass casket made for her by her fairy Godmother.

The King, Queen, Irish, Candy, and soldiers traveled to the house of Eva where she was laid on a glass casket by her mother as informed by Irish to them

Once the Queen reached there, the king opened the lid of the casket and Queen kept the flower on Eva with an apology.

Immediately there was sudden magic around Eva and up she was. She hugged the queen for accepting Ogres and Giants. The king and Queen realized their mistake that Eva never meant harm to them.

Now Greenland was a place full of peace, harmony, and love with Human Fairies, Giants, and Ogres all living together.

Go Magic and Spread happiness today ?

Contents